ETERNITY

Ellen Heiberg (trans. Lisa Freeman)

Michael Bojesen

EDITION WILHELM HANSEN

ETERNITY

Ellen Heiberg
Trans.: Lisa Freeman

Michael Bojesen 1998

Find a stone that glis - tens when you walk on the shore ____ One rolled through-out the a - ges by the o - cean's might - y roar.

WH30582

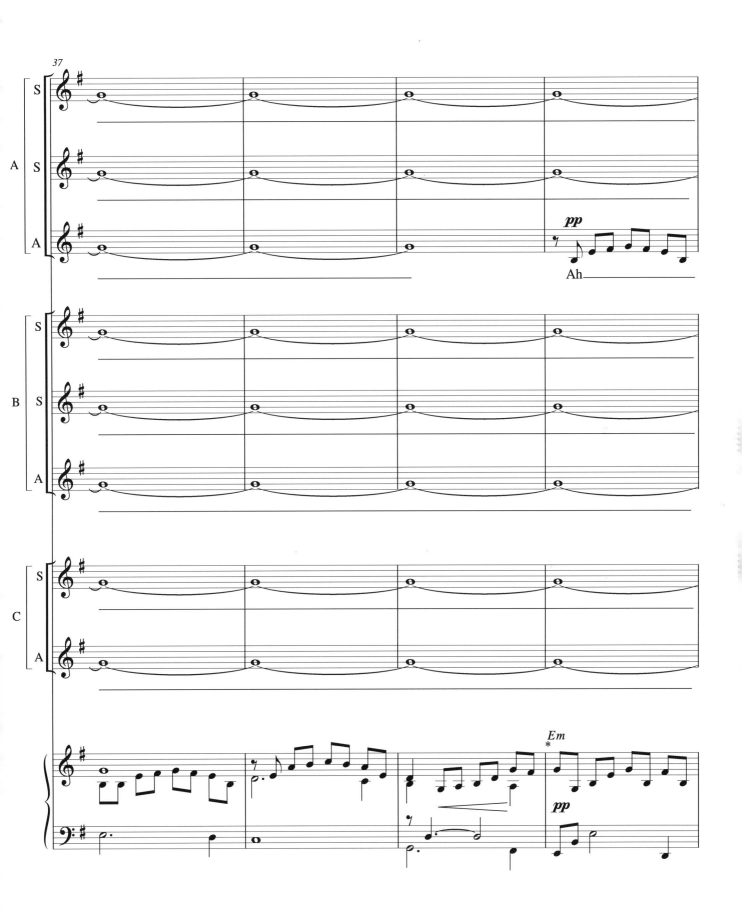

* The piano accompaniment increases and develops little by little. Improvise freely on the given chords

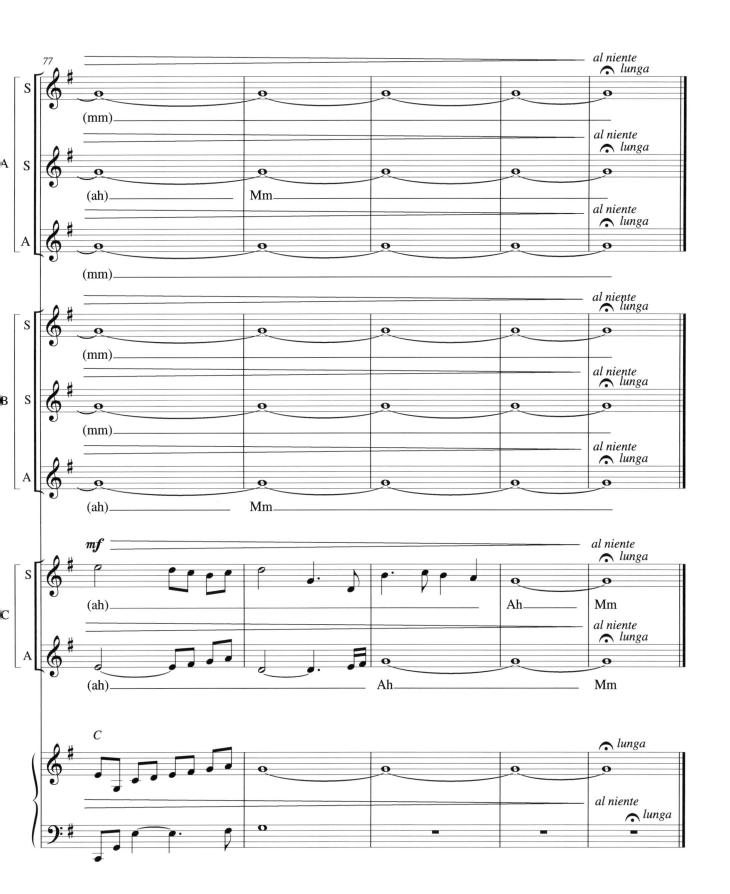